Responsibility

Written by **Ruth Percival**
Illustrated by **Dean Gray**

Published in 2026 by Windmill Books,
an Imprint of Rosen Publishing
2544 Clinton St.
Buffalo, NY 14224

First published in Great Britain in 2024 by Hodder & Stoughton
Copyright © Hodder & Stoughton Limited, 2024

Credits
Series Editor: Amy Pimperton
Series Designer: Peter Scoulding
Consultant: Philippa Anderson
Philippa Anderson has a business degree and is a writer
and communications consultant who advises multinationals.
She authors and contributes to business books.

Cataloging-in-Publication Data

Names: Percival, Ruth, author. | Grey, Dean, illustrator.
Title: Responsibility / Ruth Percival, illustrated by Dean Grey.
Description: Buffalo, NY : Windmill Books, 2026. | Series: Little business books | Includes glossary and index.
Identifiers: ISBN 9781725396555 (pbk.) | ISBN 9781725396562 (library bound) | ISBN 9781725396579 (ebook)
Subjects: LCSH: Social responsibility of business--Juvenile literature. | Entrepreneurship--Moral and ethical aspects--Juvenile literature. | Success in business--Juvenile literature.
Classification: LCC HD60.P478 2026 | DDC 338.04083--dc23

All rights reserved.

All facts and statistics were up to date at the time of press.

No part of this book may be reproduced in any form without permission
in writing from the publisher, except by a reviewer.

Printed in the United States of America

CPSIA Compliance Information: Batch #CSWM26
For Further Information contact Rosen Publishing at 1-800-237-9932

Contents

4	What Is Responsibility?
6	Be Careful with Money
8	Be Safe
10	Keep Promises
12	Be Fair
14	Don't Forget
16	Don't Copy Ideas
18	Tell the Truth
20	Say Sorry for Mistakes
22	Include Everyone
24	Be on Time
26	Help Your Community
28	Be More Eco-friendly
30	Responsibility and You
31	Notes for Sharing This Book
32	Glossary

What Is Responsibility?

Responsibility is when you are trusted to do or be in charge of something. You show responsibility through your behavior or actions.

Taking care of your toys shows you are responsible for your things. Brushing your teeth shows that you are responsible for your body. Feeding a family pet shows responsibility for others.

Sometimes, responsibility can feel difficult. You might want to have fun instead of doing your schoolwork. But doing responsible things helps you to be more grown up.

WHY IS RESPONSIBILITY IMPORTANT?

In business, responsibility is important. Responsibility can help a business to keep customers safe, pay people on time, or learn from mistakes.

For you, responsibility might mean keeping a promise. Or it might even mean helping to keep the planet clean!

What will our animal friends find out about responsibility in business and about themselves?

Be Careful with Money

Kiki Koala bought a fancy new sign for her tree farm. But now she doesn't have enough money to pay her bills.

A budget helps Kiki Koala to be more responsible. Every month, she puts aside money for bills. She saves up to buy new things for her business, too!

Being careful with money is very responsible.

Be Safe

Pip Penguin forgot to check if her ice rink is safe to skate on.

Suddenly, Leon Lion falls through a huge crack in the ice!

Oh, no!

Yikes!

Sorry, Leon, this is my fault.

Pip Penguin takes responsibility and makes a new safety rule: check the ice rink every day.

Being safe shows responsibility to yourself and others.

Keep Promises

Omar Owl promised to make a customer lots of kites for a kite festival. But Omar is worried.

Omar Owl doesn't want to let his customer down. He works extra hard to make all the kites.

Fantastic!

His customer is delighted and the kite festival is spectacular!

If you make a promise, try your best to keep it.

Be Fair

Oops! At Monkey Adventures, Milly Monkey mixed up her team's wages. Now, Kit Kangaroo knows that Omar Owl gets paid more than her.

That's not fair! I work just as hard as Omar.

Don't Forget

Peter Panda needs cheese to make pizzas in his restaurant, but the cheese shop won't deliver any today.

Peter Panda zooms to the cheese shop.
He pays his bill and buys more cheese.

I'll pay on time in the future.

Peter zips back to his restaurant, just in time ...

Remember to do important things on time.

Don't Copy Ideas

Peggy Polar Bear is about to sell her latest ice sculpture, but something is making her feel worried.

Peggy Polar Bear realizes she has done something wrong.

I copied Kiki Koala's sign!

Peggy decides to make Enzo Elephant a new sculpture. This time, the idea is all her own!

Copying ideas isn't fair to others.

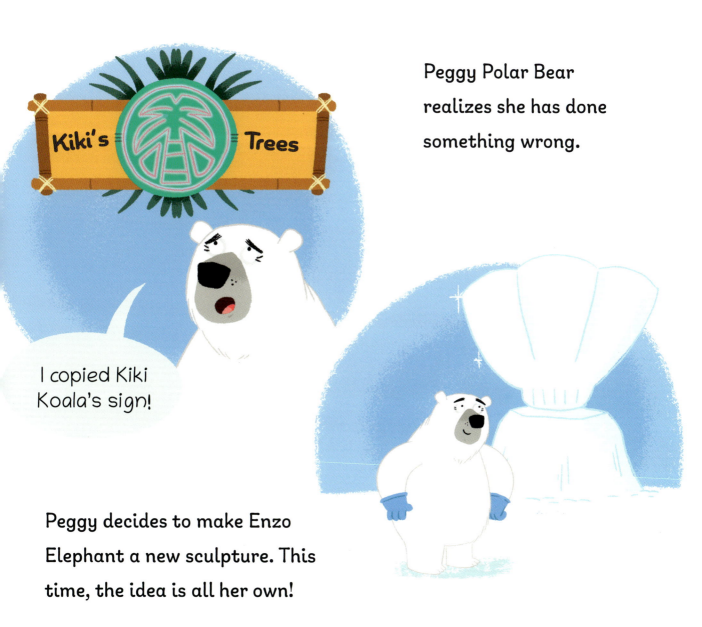

Tell the Truth

Chip Cheetah's car is being fixed at Leon Lion's car garage.

But Chip's car is still broken.

When Chip Cheetah finds out that
Leon Lion wasn't telling the truth, he is upset.

And Leon learns a lesson that telling lies is bad for his business.

Telling the truth is always the right thing to do.

Say Sorry for Mistakes

Milly Monkey ordered Wei Wolf a surprise birthday cake from Kit Kangaroo's café. The next day, Milly picks up the cake.

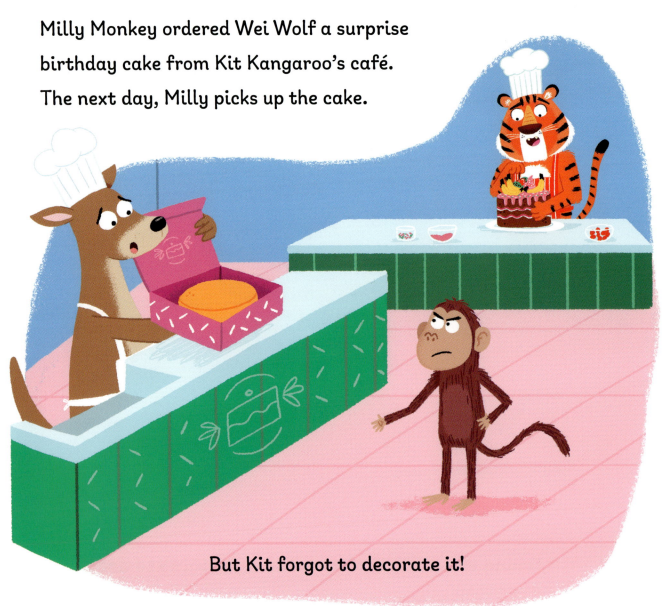

But Kit forgot to decorate it!

Kit Kangaroo thinks about blaming Tilly Tiger for the mistake. But she knows that isn't fair or kind. So Kit owns up.

Owning up to a mistake is a responsible way to behave.

Include Everyone

Wei Wolf makes hats and T-shirts.
But his products don't fit everyone.

Wei realizes that he will have more customers if he makes sizes to include everyone.

Now Wei Wolf has lots of happy customers.
And including everyone makes Wei feel happy, too.

Including everyone is responsible and kind.

Be on Time

Chip Cheetah is late – again. When he finally gets to his yoga studio, he has a lot of very unhappy customers.

But sorry isn't good enough. Chip doesn't want his business to fail. So he takes responsibility and is never late again.

Being on time is a simple way to show responsibility.

Help Your Community

The wind has blown trash all over the animals' town. They are very cross. When Enzo Elephant gets to work, he sees where the trash came from – his toy shop!

This is my responsibility.

Enzo Elephant starts picking up his trash. When the other animals see how much Enzo cares about the community, they join in and help, too.

Picking up trash safely is responsible. It shows you care about your community.

Be More Eco-friendly

Tilly Tiger holds a team meeting at Tiger Sneakers.

She wants ideas to make her business more eco-friendly.

These are all great ideas. And Tilly thinks her customers will agree. Now they can buy shoes that do less damage to the world.

We are all responsible for caring about the world we live in.

Responsibility and You

Our animal friends have learned a lot about responsibility in business. What they have learned can help you to be responsible, too.

Leon Lion found out that it is important to tell the truth. When you tell the truth you make a responsible choice.

Kit Kangaroo said sorry. Saying sorry for a mistake is an easy way to take responsibility – and it's kind, too.

Tilly Tiger helped the planet. Caring for our world is a huge responsibility that feels very rewarding.

Notes for Sharing This Book

This book introduces business ideas around the topic of responsibility, which link to core personal and social growth skills, such as how we treat others, honesty, and awareness of danger.

Talk to the child about what business is and why we need good businesses. You can use each scenario to discuss themes of responsibility. For example, you could talk about the child's feelings at a time when they were reprimanded for being late.

The more responsible you are, the more people will trust you to do things by yourself. Talk about a time when the child was trusted with a responsible task, such as looking after a class pet. What did they like best about being responsible?

Glossary

actions the things that you do; the way you behave toward others

behavior the way you act (such as using good or bad manners), especially toward others

bills documents that show how much money you owe for goods or services

budget a document to keep a record of how much money a business earns, spends, and saves

business a company that buys, makes, or sells goods or services to make money

community a group of people who live in the same place, such as a village or an area of a town or city

customer someone who buys things from a business

eco-friendly not harmful to the environment

kite festival an outdoor event where people watch lots of kites flying and performing tricks

wages the money that a business pays to its employees (people who work for a business)